OPPOSITES

By Caroline and John Astrop

BREAKWATER

big   small

Find all the big things.
Then find all the small things.

up   down

Which things are up?
Which things are down?

fat thin

Which are the fat things?
Which are the thin things?

fast slow

Which things are fast?
Which things are slow?

long   short

Which things are short?
Which things are long?

hard soft

**Which things are hard?
Which things are soft?**

clean dirty

**Can you find all the dirty things?
Can you find all the clean things?**

front   back

**Which things are showing their backs?
Which are facing the front?**

sit stand

Who are sitting?
Who are standing?

left   right

**Which things are going to the right?
Which things are going to the left?**

Look at these pictures and say the opposites.

What opposites can you find in this picture?